Business Strategies
and
Value Chain Management

Business Strategies
and
Value Chain Management

Lucas Wiedemann

authorHOUSE®

AuthorHouse™
1663 Liberty Drive
Bloomington, IN 47403
www.authorhouse.com
Phone: 1-800-839-8640

Published by AuthorHouse   03/21/2013

ISBN: 978-1-4817-8602-7 (sc)
ISBN: 978-1-4817-8603-4 (e)

Contents

Introduction

Dear Reader

The understanding of various business processes and of the concept of value chain management is a fundamental key to success and to determine the right strategy. Choosing the appropriate strategy is about as important as the selection of services and products for a company.

Each strategy has the consequence that a major administrative expense is connected and affects the flexibility of a business to a large extent. Even with the option of a version that provides a great freedom in each of the areas is very important that all activities may be monitored and set in some way.

One must be aware that each strategy comes with inherent risks and the need to weigh the risks versus the benefits must be very carefully and structured. The value chain management arising require a clear definition and control. Last but not least depends on the quality and the efficient use of resources from and a high quality today is a fundamental factor for the success of a company.

In this book I would like to make you familiar with the factors and the risks associated with the choice of business strategy. In a second step, I will occupy myself with the General values and the difficulty in controlling the building of value chain management.

This book does not claim to be exhaustive, it come me to get an insight into the topic of business processes and value chain management.

I hope you enjoy the read.

Lucas Wiedemann

1. Business management strategy

The art, science and craft of decision-making

There are some points which are relevant for a global acting company to be successful on the market and to achieve the strategic goals.

Three main strategies are used for the following areas
- Responsiveness and local differentiation
- Global scale efficiencies
- Transfer and knowledge

Three used models of company organization for the following sizes
- Multinational
- International
- Global

Three distinct management cultures
- Family
- Group
- Professional

The points can be kept with the following scheme
➢ B Business strategy
➢ O Organization model
➢ M Management cultures

The right business strategy brings the following benefits
- Evaluating the strategic options for expand overseas
- Adopting a sound business strategy for succeed as a global business

1.1 Responsiveness and differentiation
Responsiveness is the **re-action** on the behavior of the competition, the second part of an action
- Responsiveness to local market needs (local market usage)
- Sensitivity to local and regional government regulation
- Responsiveness to local competitors

◉ Customer service orientation

1.2 Global scale efficiencies
This is the global presentation of a global acting company
☺ Benefits

◉ Manufacturing scale
◉ R + D marketing scale
◉ Speed of execution of customer's need

globally production
globally research and
 development activity
faster re-action

1.3 Transfer of knowledge
Concentrates on boosting the innovation level of a company's subsidiaries. It is carried in four stages

1. Export early generation products (direct export from the parent company)
◉ When the product is not stable and it is difficult for the local subsidiary to obtain the knowledge from the parent company

2. Manufacture the same products in local subsidiaries
◉ Once the manufacturing process is established at the parent company, the local staff are trained to replicate the manufacturing process

3. Develop products adapted to local markets
◉ Once the local staff is enough trained and has the necessary skills, the transfer of knowledge can begin.

4. Develop new products based on new technologies
◉ Shared learning

2. Organization model

The distinguished characteristics are part of each of the three models
- Arrangements of assets and capabilities
- Role of overseas operations
- Development and transfer of knowledge

The understanding of various organizational models has the following advantages

- Understanding how global companies organize their overseas subsidiaries
- Understanding the management issues and practices of different organization models

Each of this organization model helps to achieve one of the strategic objectives, especially

Multinational Model   Responsiveness
International Model      Transfer of knowledge
Global   Global Scale Efficiency

2.1   Multinational model
In a Multinational model the headquarters are set up in different countries.

Characteristics

- Independent national entities
- A portfolio of multiple national entities
- Sensing and exploiting local opportunities for each of the entity
- Knowledge is developed within each parent or subsidiary unit

2.2   International model
In an International model, the headquarter has a strong influence on the subsidiaries.
Characteristics

- The main task is to transfer knowledge and skills to overseas markets
- The subsidiaries are more dependent on the parent through close coordination and communication
- Technology development is controlled by the parent and transferred to its overseas units
- Subsidiaries take the responsibility to adapt and leverage the parent competences
- Responsibilities and decisions are controlled by headquarter

2.3   Global model
Characteristics
- The world market is treated as an integrated whole
- Central control of assets, resources and responsibilities
- The subsidiary of a global company relies on its parent company for business strategies
- The role of the subsidiary is limited to sale and service
- Knowledge is developed at the parent companies, it is not transferred to the subsidiary

2.4   Transnational model
The transnational model is a mixture of all the models shown above. This means it can contain parts of the following organization models

- Multinational model   regarding the responsiveness
                                                              and differentiation
- International model   regarding the transfer or
                                                              knowledge
- Global   regarding the global scale
                                                              efficiency

3. Cultural efficiencies in business management

Three management cultures have emerged as a dominant role
- Family management culture
- Group management culture
- Professional management culture

Benefits of understanding the different cultures
- Understand the critical role that culture plays
- Recognizing the relationship between cultural tendencies and organizational structure

3.1   Family management culture (multinational)
The following points are the characteristics of this culture type
- Family members or trusted persons are often sent to manage overseas operations
- Multinational model orientation
- Loose management controls
- Subsidiaries managed as investment portfolios

3.2   Group management culture (global)
The following points are the characteristics of this culture type
- Group conformity, following group norms
- All decisions are made by consensus
- Global model orientation
- Intense management control, mistrust of outsiders
- Emphasizing group harmony

3.3   Professional management culture (international)
The following points are the characteristics of this culture type
- Professionals are hired as managers to run the company
- Separation between ownership and management
- International model orientation
- Well-defined systematic controls, provides a regular flow of management

3.4   Corporate heritage and cultural tendencies
The company heritage affects its ability to succeed in the global business environment

Corporate heritage is developed by the following factors
- Political factors
- Cultural trends
- Technological development
- Historical factors

3.4.1 Historical factors
European companies are mostly organized multinational
- Long history of economics of scale
- Pre-war political pressure for decentralization

US-companies are organized international
- Large home market
- Strong technology and capabilities of headquarters

Japanese companies are organized global

4. Technology management strategy

There are some common strategies regarding technology management

- CTM   Centralized Technology Management
- LTM   Local Technology Management
- GTM   Globally coordinated Technology Management
- SA   Strategic Alliance

Three key factors are essential for the correct and corresponding strategy
- Technological expertise
- Market acceptance
- Evaluating R+D costs

4.1 Centralized technology management (global)
Used by global operating companies with a centralized structure.
Benefits
- Establishing global companies with centralized structure
- Promoting a sense of belonging among staff
- Building commitment to company, plans and assets

Characteristics of CTM
- Technology is completely driven and managed by a centralized group in a centralized location
- Uniform marketing approach
- Strong emphasis on product standardization to achieve global economics of scale
- Limited functions of subsidiaries

Substantiation for the use of CTM
Benefits
- Protection of key technology assets
- Integration of multiple disciplines
- Maintain focus on overall business strategy
- Speed of development

Possible risks
- Insensitivity to local markets needs
- Inability to respond to local competition
- Lack of product knowledge by the local marketing/sales staff

4.1.1 The CTM best practices

Three organizational mechanisms that are particularly important for successful CTM
- Multiple linkages
    - ✓ Instead of restricted communication, ideas and information are channeled directly from departments in various subsidiaries to relevant departments at headquarters
- Internal market mechanisms
    - ✓ This mechanism gives subsidiaries an opportunity to select for their own markets the product and technology developed at headquarters
- Personnel flows
    - ✓ Each staff has the opportunity to step up in his career

Only used for proprietary knowledge

4.2 Local technology management (multinational)

This is strategy for global operating businesses in which local managers are responsible for product and marketing, according to the local market.

Characteristics of LTM
- Minimal intervention from headquarters
- Multinational model
- Subsidiaries develop products for their own market
- Technologies are developed and managed locally
- Subsidiaries have their own local staff
- Overall financial control is made by the parent company
- Competition among subsidiaries
- The parent company has little control over technologies developed by the subsidiaries
- Senior management and other critical positions at subsidiaries are mainly composed of local professionals

Substantiation for the use of LTM

Benefits

- Respond effectively to local market needs
- Succeed in markets critical to the business
- Make full use of local expertise and technology

Possible risks

- Development efforts may be duplicated
- Innovations may not be widely leveraged
- Returns on R+D investments may be limited

4.2.1   LTM best practices

- Empowering local management
- Local organizations must be given significant authority to manage and control their assets and resources
   - ✓ Linking corporate decision-making processes
- LTM-oriented companies can build linkage between its local subsidiaries between objectives and those of the parent company
   - ✓ Integrating technical and marketing functions at local operations
- A company speeds up the decision-making process for its local business

4.3   Globally coordinated technology management

A business strategy that combine factors of local and central management

Characteristics of GTM

- The headquarter coordinates the development of technologies at its various subsidiaries
- The company leverages the talents, resources, market opportunities and capabilities of every global location
- Enhancement of the overall effectiveness of a company's development activities and local market know-how at each of its global locations
- Staff frequently move among the various company locations
- Close communication and coordination exists between local subsidiaries and headquarters
- Managers respond to both local and entire company needs

Substantiation for the use of GTM

Benefits

- Realize the importance of knowing both the central goal and the local goal of the company
- Become aware of the need to maximize the use of technology innovation
- Maximize the financial returns on R+D investments

Possible risks

- Cultural and language differences
- Higher coordination costs
- Ambiguity in execution

4.3.1 GTM best practices

- Inter-dependence of resources and responsibilities I
  - ✓ The organizational structure be based on a principle of reciprocal dependences among the subsidiaries
  - ✓ Each subsidiary follows its own interests
- Inter unit integration devices
  - ✓ Controlled operating systems
  - ✓ A people-linking process
  - ✓ Inter-unit forums
  - ✓ Central control of key strategic operation elements
- National competitors and global perspective

4.4 Strategic alliances

- Reduces the enormous costs of R+D
- Collaboration between companies
  - ✓ Joint venture
  - ✓ Product licensing
  - ✓ Outsourcing agreement
  - ✓ Corporate research

Characteristics of strategic alliances

- Partners have specific strategic objectives to achieve
- Partners complete and compete with each other
- Partners focus on learning from each other

- Each company must select specific skills to transfer to the partner while preserving the capacity to retain key's competitive advantages

Substantiation for the use of SA
Benefits
- Speed in marketing
- Combined power
- Complementary benefits
- Potential risk prevention

4.4.1 Management concerns in strategic alliances
The following concerns must be taken into account before a strategic alliance will be discussed
- Protection of key assets and personnel
- Learning from partner
  - ✓ Hold regular meetings to let employees share knowledge acquired from partners
  - ✓ Conduct training programs on specific topics and pre-specified time intervals
  - ✓ Assign managers to oversee any training efforts that involve the partner
- Clarity of objectives
  - ✓ Articulate the concrete goals
- Managing the relationship

5. Strategic Management

The Strategic Management is characterized by the following features
This is a set of decisions and actions that result in the formulation and
implementation of plans, designed to achieve a company's objectives

Two parts are the basic elements for the strategic management.
- Planning
  - ✓ Defining the company mission, goals
  - ✓ Performing an internal analysis, resources
  - ✓ Evaluating the external environment, strategic options

- Implementation
  - ✓ Long term objectives and grand strategies
  - ✓ Strategic analysis and choice
  - ✓ Action plans and functional tactics
  - ✓ Strategy institutionalization
  - ✓ Strategic control and improvement

Benefits of the strategic management, it can help by
- The firm's ability to prevent problems is enhanced
- Group-based strategic decisions are often drawn from the best available alternatives
- Employees involvement in strategy formulation helps to heighten their motivation
- Gaps and overlaps in activities among individuals and groups are reduced
- Resistance to change is reduced

5.1 Characteristics of strategic decisions
- They require top-management decisions
- Involvement in large amounts of company resources
- Takes a long time for a strategy in taking full effect
- Have multifunctional consequences
- Focused on the firm's future development
- Requires a consideration of a firm's external environment

5.2 Levels of strategic management

There are some levels characteristic for the strategic management

Corporate level (board of directors, CEO), they are responsible for the following actions
- Financial performance
- Public image
- Social responsibility

Business level (Business and corporate manager)
- Competitive advantage

Functional level
- Implement of higher-level decisions
- Annual objectives
- Short-term strategies

The scope of the formality which is needed depends from
- The size of the company
- The firms predominant management cycle
- The complexity of the firm's environment
- The production process of the firm
- The purpose of the firm's planning system

5.3 Components of strategic management planning
- Defining the company mission
- Performing an internal analysis
- External environment

5.3.1 The component of external environment can be divided into three parts
- Remote environment
  - ✓ Economic
  - ✓ Social
  - ✓ Political
  - ✓ Technological
  - ✓ Ecological

- Industry environment
  - ✓ Thread of new entrants
  - ✓ Bargaining power of customers
  - ✓ Bargaining power of suppliers
  - ✓ Thread of substitutes
  - ✓ Jockeying among current contestants

- Operating environment
  - ✓ Obtain needed resources
  - ✓ Selling the goods and services

5.4 Viewing strategic management as a process

For understanding the strategic management, please take care
It's essential to look at the strategic management as a process. This means that
- A change in any component will affect several or all of the other components
- Strategy formulations and implementations are sequential
- The necessity of feedback from institutionalization, review and evaluation to the early stages of the process
- The need to regard strategic management as dynamic system

5.4.1 Defining the company mission

First step, define the company mission
It describes the firm product, market and technological focus and thereby reflects the values and priorities of the firm's strategic decision makers.

The following six outcomes must be achieved
- Build an unified purpose within the company
- Direct and motivate the allocation of company's resources
- Establish an organizational climate
- Inform people of the company's purpose and direction
- Provide a basis for the assignment of work
- Guide the development of control and assessment practices

Benefits of a clear mission statement
- Give managers clear direction
- Build common understanding among all employees

- Communicate the company values and purposes to concerned parties
- Affirm the company's commitment to socially responsible practices

5.4.2 Components of a company mission
- Company business activity
  - ✓ Specified basic product or services
  - ✓ Specified primary market
  - ✓ Specified principal technology for production and delivery

- Company goals
  - ✓ Survival
  - ✓ Profitability
  - ✓ Growth

- Company philosophy
  - ✓ Basic belief
  - ✓ Values
  - ✓ Aspiration

- Public image
  - ✓ Certain qualities expected from customers

- Company self concept
  - ✓ Weak and strengths of a company
  - ✓ The firms impact on others and others impact on the firm

Two new components from some firms
- Consumer
  - ✓ Consumer needs before and after a sale

- Quality

5.5 Stakeholder approach to company responsibility
Definition
A stakeholder is a person or a group who is engaged or affected by any action of a company.

There are two groups of stakeholders

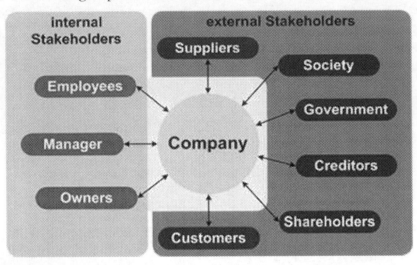

- Internal stakeholders
    - ✓ Owners
    - ✓ Management
    - ✓ Employees

- Outside stakeholders
    - ✓ Customer
    - ✓ Shareholders
    - ✓ Creditors
    - ✓ Suppliers
    - ✓ Society
    - ✓ Government

The following steps are needed to attempt the stakeholders interest
- Identify the stakeholder
- Understand the stakeholders specific claims
- Reconcile and assign priorities to these claims
- Coordinate the claims with other elements of the company mission

5.6   Internal analysis
Definition
The internal analysis is needed for achieving the following goals

- Provides a foundation for strategic formulation
- Develops a company profile that reflects the internal conditions

For developing a company profile the SWOT analysis a useful tool to get needed information

SWOT Analysis
- Provides managers with an overview of a firm's strategic position
  - ✓ Internal capabilities
  - ✓ External situation

The strategy is influenced by these both factors

S	Strength	supports a diversification strategy
W	Weaknesses	support a turnaround-oriented strategy
O	Opportunities	supports an aggressive strategy
T	Threat	the entry of new competitor

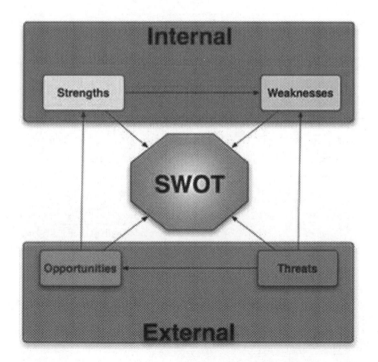

Typical internal factors in various functional areas
- Marketing
- Financial and accounting
- Production, operations, technical
- Personnel
- Quality management
- IT
- General management

Functional approaches in SWOT

- Analyzing a company's location of facilities
- Examine a company's raw material costs

These activities are divided along functional lines

Comparison standards of internal analysis
- Post performance
- Competitors
- Industry success and stage of evolution

Stage of evolution
The stage of evolution consists of the following phases

Phase 1 Introduction   low profit, few competitors,
                                                  high cost
Phase 2 Growth   high profit, many competitors,
                                                  low cost
Phase 3 Maturity   stable profit but less, many
                                                  competitors, stable cost
Phase 4 Decline   low profit, low cost

5.7   External environment
These consist of 3 factors
- Remote environment factors
- Industry environment factors
- Operating environment factors

5.7.1   Remote environment
Definition

These are factors outside its operating situations

A single firm rarely has the power to affect the remote environment

Five factors build the remote environment

- Economic
- Social
- Political
- Technological
- Ecological

Economic factors

- Industry economic factors, economic trends
- National and international factors, credit availability, the level of disposable income
- Other economic factors, prime interest rates and trends in the growth of gross national product

Social factors

- Beliefs
- Values
- Attitudes
- Opinions and lifestyle

Political factors

- Legal and regulatory parameters

Technical factors

- Aware of technological advances that might influence its industry

5.7.2   Industry environment
Factors

The industry company is confronted with the following risk in its environment

- Threat of new entrants
- Bargaining power of suppliers
- Bargaining power of customers
- Threat of substitute products or services
- Jockeying among current contestants (contending forces)

Threat of new entrants
The following factors can bring a new entrant to the market
- Desire to gain market share
- Substantial resources
- New capacity

Bargaining power of suppliers
- Price limitation,
- Domination
- Competition

Bargaining power of customers
- Price decreases
- Demand higher quality
- Demand more service

Consequences
The power of suppliers and the power of customers in its different have all the same consequence

- Consequence   profit limitation

Market situations
Whether a buyer group is powerful is determined by seven market situations
- Large volume buying
- Standard products
- Favourable prices
- Low profits earning
- Quality importance
- Not saving the buyer money
- Integration

Jockeying among current contestants
The type of competition is related to a number of factors
- Numerous competitors to the market
- Slow industry growth
- Less differentiated products or services
- Higher fixed costs or perishable products

- Augmented capacity in large increments
- High exit barrier
- Diversification of rivals in strategies, origins and personalities

5.7.2.1 Industry and competitive analysis
Different kinds of analysis
- What are the boundaries of the industry
- What is the structure of the industry
- Which firms are competitors in the industry

Industry boundary
- Industrial evolution creates opportunities and threats
- Industrial evolution creates industries within industries
- Industries are becoming more global in scope

Starting point for drawing industry boundaries
- Part of the industry that is a firm's main business
- Ingredients key for success in specific business areas
- Skills needed for competition
- Flexibility to adjust business concept

Industry structure
- Concentration
- Economic of scale
- Product differentiation
- Barriers to entry

Industry competitors
- Other firms' definition of their market scope
- Similarity of benefits to customers from other firms
- Commitment of other firms to the industry

5.7.3 Operating environment
- Competitive position
- Composition of customers
- Reputation among suppliers
- Reputation among creditors
- Attraction to capable employees

Competitive position

Factors for rating the competitive position
- Market share and broth of product line
- Effectiveness of sale distribution and promotion
- Proprietary and key account advantages
- Price competiveness
- Location and age of facility
- Capacity and productivity
- Raw material costs
- Financial and R+D advantages position
- Calibre of personnel

Customer profile

Factors for making a customer profile
- Geographic
- Demographic
- Psychographic
- Buyer behaviour

Relationship between a firm and its suppliers

Several key issues
- Supplier competitive prices or attractive quantities discounts
- Less costly shipping charges or suppliers who are competitive in terms of production standards
- Suppliers competitive abilities, reputations and services in terms of deficiency rates
- Suppliers who are reciprocally dependent on the firm

Relationship between firm and its creditors
- Have creditors a strong working capital
- Have creditors the ability to extend the necessary line of credit

Possibility for companies

Firm's ability to attract and retrain employees
- Firm's reputation
- Local employment rates
- Availability of needed people

5.8   Environmental factors

- Select the environmental variables
- Select the sources of environmental information
- Evaluate forecasting techniques
- Integrate forecast results into strategic management
- Monitor the critical aspects of managing forecasts

Forecast techniques

- Economic forecast
- Econometric forecast
- Social forecast
- Political forecast
- Technological forecast

6. Strategic management analysis and choice

The different strategies

Long-term objectives	describes the results a company seeks to achieve at some time in the future
Generic strategies	helps the company create important advantages over their competitors
Grand strategies	give you the basic directions you need to achieve long-term objectives

6.1   Long-term objectives and grand strategies
- Study the opportunities
- Decide which long-term objectives are most likely to be achieved
- Evaluate the types of strategies that will also take advantage of your competitors

6.1.1   Long-term objectives
Possible application

You can identify the best use of your resources and profits to achieve long-term prosperity

The span consist a wide range of activities
- Profitability
- Productivity
- Competitive position
- Employee development
- Employer relation
- Technological leadership
- Public responsibility

Key for using

Seven criteria are the key to develop well-defined long-term objectives
- Acceptable
- Flexible
- Measurable over time
- Motivating
- Suitable

- Understandable
- Achievable

Acceptable
The LTO must be acceptable for the key external groups, incl. the employees

Flexible
Must be adaptable to unexpected events or changes

Measurable
Must provide specific benchmark for evaluating a company's progress in achieving its aims

Motivating
Must be high enough to challenge but not so high that it is frustrating or so low that it is easily achieved

Suitable
It must be suitable to the company mission

Understandable
The objectives are clear and unambiguous

6.2   Generic strategies
Definition
This is the strategic planning by any firm in any market to improve its competitive performance

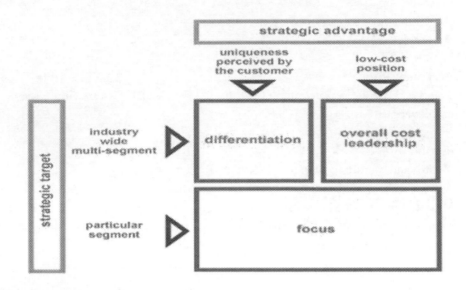

- Sustain low-cost position
- Defend itself on price wars
- Attack competitors on price to increase market share
- Simply enjoy exceptional returns
- Leaders in cost reductions and efficiencies
    - ✓ Utilizing cost-cutting technologies
    - ✓ Achieving economics of scale
    - ✓ Cutting overhead and administrative expenses
    - ✓ Using volume-based marketing techniques

Differentiation
- Set the product or services clearly apart from those of the competitors
- Sophisticated marketing channels through which the product is delivered
- An image of excellence
- Special features included in the product
- A strong service network that supports the product
- Higher profits
- Brand loyalty of the customer
- Creative ideas
- A good relationship with suppliers

Focus
- Concentrate on specific market segments

6.3   Traditional grand strategies
- Concentrated growth, increasing market share
- Market development
- Product development
- Innovation, new products
- Horizontal integration, acquisition of competitors
- Vertical integration, acquisition of suppliers
- Concentric diversification
- Conglomerate diversification
- Turnaround, reduce costs, asset, changes in top-management
- Divestiture, sale of either the whole firm or a major component
- Liquidation

Market development
- Adding distribution channel
- Changing advertisement content
- Expanding geographically

Product development
- Prolong the life cycle of current products
- Take advantage of an established reputation or brand loyalty

Concentric diversification
- Spin-off of a separate business
- Value chains are related to and compatible with the acquiring firm

Conglomerate diversification
- Spin-off of a separate business
- Value chains are not related to and not compatible with the acquiring firm

6.3.1 New grand strategies—corporate combinations
- Joint venture
- Strategic alliance
- Consortia

Joint venture
A third commercial company created and operated for the benefit of the co-owners

Strategic alliance
There are no ownership position in the other company. They are formed through licensing agreements and outsourcing

Five reasons for outsourcing
- Improved business focus
- Access to worldwide capabilities
- Accelerated re-engineering benefits
- Shared risks
- Free resources for other purposes

Consortia
A large interlocking relationship between businesses within the same industry

7. Strategic analysis and choice

Possible application
Examining and selecting business strategies

- C   competitive advantage
- I   industry environments
- A   additional considerations

The importance of strategic analysis and choice
- Helps a company to identify the source of competitive advantage that best suits the company
- Enables a company to select a proper business strategy that positions the company most effectively in its industry

7.1   Sources of competitive advantages (C)
- Cost leadership, reduces the likelihood of pricing pressure, lessens the attractiveness of substitutes
- Differentiation, decreases buyers' interest to prices, reduces rivalry among competitors
- Speed
- Market focus

7.1.1 Risks of cost leadership
- Adaption of competitors
- Oversight of other advantages
- Loss of value on products
- Imitation by other companies

7.1.2 Risks of differentiation
- Failure caused by product imitation
- Malediction of investment plans with innovations
- Buyers' preference to low-cost products

7.1.3 Speed
Prerequisites
To get speed advantage a business must have the following trails
- Highly automated technical skills
- Balanced control of inside and outside issues
- Good relationship with partners and suppliers

Advantages to speed
- Quick response to customer requests
- Improving product quality and services
- Speed in obtaining updated IT
- Quick delivery of products to customer

How to get advantages
- Exclusive access to resources
- High prices on products
- Exclusion of competitors

7.2 Industry environment and strategic choices (I)
Definition
The industry environment is the set of factors—the threat of new entrants, suppliers, buyers, product substitutes, and the intensity of rivalry among competitors—that directly influences a firm and its competitive actions and responses.

The industry environment can be divided in 5 parts.
- Emerging industries
- Maturing industries
- Declining industries
- Fragmental industries
- Global industries

Each industry begins with the emerging stage.

7.2.1 Emerging industries
This is an industry, usually formed by a new idea or a new product
There are several strategies to evaluate to be successful

- Shape the new industry structure
- Quickly improve product quality and build the dominant technology
- Establish an advantageous relationship with the key suppliers and main buyers
- Be aware of future competitors and their possible strategies

7.2.2 Maturing industries
An industry which has the emerging and the growth phases of industry growth

Strategies to become more competitive
- Cost reduction, obtaining cheaper raw materials
- Selection of customers
- Expansion of business

7.2.3 Declining industries
An industry where growth is either negative or is not growing at the broader rate of economic growth.
Strategies to become more competitive
- Focus on markets that might present higher profits
- Develop new products efficiently
- Increase product quality and distribution speed
- Create capital by lowering maintenance fees

7.2.4 Fragmental industries
Many firms share markets for professional services, distribution and agricultural products.
Strategies to pursue competitive advantages
- Lightly managed decentralisation, local management
- Formula facilities
- Increased value added
- Specialized
- Bare bones / no frills

Formula facilities
- A way to build effective low-cost activities at multiple locations

Increased value added
- An approach that provides both service and product sales to customers

Base bones / no frills
- To have the lowest possible costs by providing low employee wages and controlling expenses tightly

7.2.5 Global industry
The ability to obtain worldwide market shares and generic competitive firms. Strategies to achieve world wide competitive advantages
- Broad line global competition
- Global focus strategy
- National focus strategy
- Protected niche strategy

7.3 Additional considerations affective strategy choices (A)
Current strategy
- External dependence
- Attitudes toward risks
  - ✓ Industry volatility
  - ✓ Industry evolution

- Internal politics
- Time concerns
  - ✓ Time limits
  - ✓ Timing

- Competitors' reactions

8. Strategic choice in different type of businesses

Grand strategy selection in single or dominant products/services
Diversification and integration in multi-business companies

8.1 Strategic choice in single product businesses
Grand strategy selection matrix
- It seeks to reduce weaknesses or maximize strengths
- It chooses between an internal or external emphasis for growth and profitability

Model of grand strategy clusters
- Its product market is growing fast or slowly
- Its competitive position is strong or weak

8.1.1 Grand strategy selection matrix
Internal opportunities ↔ External opportunities
Overcoming weakness ↕ Maximizing strength

Quadrant II Overcoming weakness Seeking internal opportunities	Quadrant I Overcoming weakness Seeking external opportunities
Quadrant III Maximizing strength Seeking internal opportunities	Quadrant IV Maximizing strength Seeking external opportunities

Strategies for quadrant I
- Vertical integration
- Conglomerate diversification

Strategies for quadrant II
- Retrenchment
- Divestiture
- Liquidation

Strategies for quadrant III
- Concentrated growth
- Innovation
- Product development
- Market development

Strategies for quadrant IV
- Horizontal integration
- Diversification
- Joint venture

8.1.2 Model of grand strategy clusters
This model is on the belief that a company's situation is defined by its market growth rate and the competitiveness of a product
Strong position ↔ Weak position
Fast growing market ↕ Slow growing market

Quadrant I Strong competitive position Fast growing market	Quadrant II Weak competitive position Fast growing market
Quadrant IV Strong competitive position Slow growing market	Quadrant III Weak competitive position Slow growing market

Strategies for quadrant I
- Vertical integration
- Concentric diversification

Strategies for quadrant II
- Formulation or reformulation of a concentrated growth strategy
- Horizontal integration
- Divestiture
- Liquidation

Strategies for quadrant III
- Retrenchment
- Liquidation
- Divestiture
- Conglomerate diversification

Strategies for quadrant IV
- Concentric diversification
- Conglomeratic diversification
- Joint venture

8.2 Strategic choice in multi-business companies
Justify integration and diversification in other interested parties
Stockholders benefit from a successful choice

8.2.1 Question 1: Are there opportunities for sharing infrastructure and capabilities
Shared opportunities are meaningful when they incorporate two elements
- The shared opportunities involve major activities in business value chain
- The business must have shared needs

8.2.2 Question 2: Are we making the most of our competencies
Core competences refer to the key value-building skills that a company possess, when their skills influence other products in a separate part of the market they create extra values.

There are three basic considerations in which deciding whether companies should capitalize on their core competencies.
- Do core competencies provide a competitive advantage for the intended businesses
- Do the intended businesses benefit from the same core competencies
- Is the combination of competencies unique

8.2.3 Question 3: Does it balance
In a multi-business company, businesses generate and use different amounts of cash
High cash generation market share ↔ Low cash generation market share

High cash use growth rate ↕ Low cash use growth rate

8.2.3.1 Cash Generating Matrix

Star High cash generation High cash use	Problem Low cash generation High cash use
Cash cow High cash generation Low cash use	Dog Low cash generation Low cash use

8.2.3.2 Business strength matrix
Horizontal
Business unit strength   Vertical
                                                Market Attractiveness

Weak   Average   Strong

Invest	Selective Growth	Grow or let go
Selective Growth	Grow or let go	Harvest
Divest	Harvest	Grow or let go

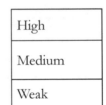

High
Medium
Weak

8.2.3.3 Life cycle competitive strength matrix

Introduction	Growth	Maturity	Decline	Cycle
PUSH Invest Aggressively				High Competitive
	CAUTION Invest Selectively			Moderate Competitive
			DANGER Harvest	Low Competitive

8.2.4 Question 4: Does our business portfolio achieve appropriate levels of risk and growth

Key concerns used to justify diversification and integration
- Balance of financial resources
- Use of core competencies
- Opportunity for sharing resources
- Reasonable levels of risk and growth

8.2.5 Four circumstances to justify considerations diversification and integration
- The company has good opportunities for sharing infrastructure and capabilities
- The company is capitalizing on its core competences
- The business portfolio balances its use of financial resources
- The business portfolio achieves suitable levels of risk and growth

9. Strategy management implementation

- Action plans + functional tactics
- Strategic integration
- Strategic control + continuous improvement
  - ✓ Track how strategies are implemented
  - ✓ Detect potential problems or changes

Make the necessary adjustments

10. Implementing strategic through business functions

- Determine action plans + short-term objectives
- Originate specific functional tactics
- Communicate policies that empower staff

Implementing strategic through business functions allows
- Translate thought into action
- Specify tasks of each functional area
- Implement grand strategies at the operational level

10.1   Action plans and short-term objectives

Effective action plans have value-added benefits
- Specific tactic and actions
- Clear time frame for completion
- Identification of personnel involved
- Short-term objectives

Well-developed short-term objectives need to have three qualities
- Measurability
- Priorities
- Linkage to long-term objectives

10.1.1 Benefits
- Provide help in handling problems that arise in implementing strategy
- Every department has a defined purpose within the organization
- They offer a foundation for strategic control
- Motivate managerial performance

10.2   Functional tactics

Functional tactics are based on grand strategies and carry out specific short-term objectives

- Functional tactics

- Grand strategies   Production / Operation
  - ✓ Marketing
  - ✓ Accounting / Finance
  - ✓ R + D
  - ✓ HR

10.2.1 POM Production Operations Management

Facilities and equipment
- How centralized do we want our facilities to be
- What is the optimal level of integration for separate processes
- How much should we further automate processes
- Will we base size and capacity decisions on normal or peak operation levels

10.2.2 Purchasing as a critical part of POM

For the right purchasing tactic consider the following factors
- Final vendors
- Priority of just in time delivery
- Operating approaches
- Overdependence on a few fixed suppliers

10.2.3 Planning and control in POM

- Should work be scheduled to build by stock or fill orders
- What is the optimal inventory level
- How do we manage our inventory
- What are the major control concerns
- What is the goal of maintenance, prevention or repair
- To what degree do we need to emphasize safety, quality standards and job specialization

There are different ways to measure value and quality
- Just in time delivery
- Outsourcing
- Statistical process control

10.2.4 Marketing
- P Product, what are our most profitable products
- P Price, what is the best price
- P Promotion, who do we sell our product
- P Place, where do we sell our product

10.2.5 Accounting and finance
Activity-based cost
- ➤ Accounting for costs of products and services
- ➤ Valuing the business, especially public traded companies

Financial tactics
- Capital acquisition
- Capital allocation
- Dividend management
- Working capital management

10.2.6 Research and development
Tactics
- Research focus
- Time horizon
- Organizational fit
- Basic R+D posture

how much basic research
short or long-term growth
in house or outsourced
aggressive or defensive

10.2.7 HR
Tactics
- Recruitment, selection and orientation
- Career, development and training
- Compensation
- Evaluation, discipline and control
- Labor relations and equal opportunity requirements

Lucas Wiedemann

10.3   Policies empowering operational personnel

It is important to empower staff members with the authority to make decisions at their own level

Policies clarify business activities for five purposes

- Provide indirect control
- Establish uniform handling
- Ensure quick decisions
- Institutionalize routine behaviour
- Resolve staff resistance, problems

11. Integrating strategy into the organization

Six components to ensure effective strategic execution
- Structure
- System
- Shared value (culture)
- Skills
- Style
- Staff

The six elements can be arranged into four groups
- Structure, the way the firm's different activities are organized
- Leadership, the way to establish an effective style to accomplish the strategy
- Culture, the value that create the norms of individual behaviour and the tone of the organization
- Rewards system, the way to reward performances and monitor organizational actions

Benefits
- Keep pace with competitive global economics
- Build and maintain effective leadership
- Gain the support of all stakeholders
- Motivate employees to do an excellent job

11.1 Types of primary organization structure
- Organizational structure
- Functional structure
- Geographic organizational structure
- Divisional structure
- Matrix organizational structure

11.1.1 Organizational structure
CEO
The CEO is responsible for the organization of the following areas
- Engineering
- Production
- Personnel
- Finance and accounting
- Marketing

11.1.2 Functional structure
Advantages
- Employees are able to develop an expertise in particular functional areas
- Efficiency is improved when employees apply new technologies

11.1.3 Geographic organizational structure
Advantages
- It allows a change of strategy to suit the needs of each geographic market
- It helps to take advantage of the economic and regional operations

Disadvantages
- Difficulty to use the same company image in different geographical areas
- Services of staff at both headquarters and district level may overlap each other

11.1.4 Divisional structure
This structure is used for
- Is used when many different product lines are existing

Advantage
- It can narrow the gap between development and implementation of the divisions

Disadvantage
- It will increase the competition for corporate level resources

Strategic business unit
- Is used to simplify the divisional structure
- Each group has a vice-president who controls more divisions
- Divisions with similar strategies are lead in business units

Advantage
- It improves the coordination between divisions in a group

Disadvantage
- In a strategic business unit the role of the group vice-president is difficult to define

11.1.5 Matrix organizational structure
- Has project managers and vice-presidents for a function
- Is organized in vertical and horizontal ways

Advantages
- Allows for a variety of project-oriented business activities
- Maximizes efficient use of functional managers

Disadvantages
- Can result in confusion and unclear policies
- Require much horizontal and vertical coordination

11.2   Selecting an effective organizational structure
- R Restructure to emphasize and support strategically critical activities
- R Reengineer strategic business processes
- D Downsize outsource and self-management
- R Reorganize the strategy and structure often evolve in a predictable pattern

11.2.1 Five different types of critical activities
- Compete as low-cost goods or service provider
- Compete as high-quality provider
- Stress customer service, rapid response
- Provide rapid and frequent introduction of new products
- Seek vertical integration

11.2.2 Business process reengineering
- Develop a flow chart of the total business process
- Simplify the process by streamlining steps and tasks
- Decide which parts can be automated
- Analyze each activity to decide which ones are critical for the strategy
- Consider the pros and cons of outsourcing non-critical activities
- Design a structure and reorganize the personnel to fit the structure

11.2.3 Downsizing
- Reduce the number of middle managers
- Self-management, more work
- Outsourcing of non-critical activities

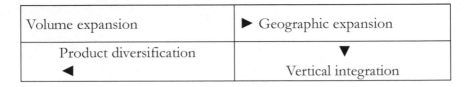

Volume expansion	► Geographic expansion
Product diversification ◄	▼ Vertical integration

11.2.4 Step-by-step development of strategy and structure
- Firms use functional structures for a dominant business
- Firms in a related diversified business use multidivisional structure
- In a unrelated diversified business, firms use strategic business unit

11.3   Leadership in an organization
- Clarify strategic intent
- Build an organization
- Shape organizational culture

11.3.1 Rebuild an organization
- Confirm that all staff know the company's priorities
- Clarify responsibilities among managers
- Empower new management
- Expose and solve problems in a cooperative manner throughout the organization
- Obtain the personal commitment to a shared vision from all the managers

- Always remember what's going on the organization and with its customers

11.3.2 Concerns of organizational leadership
Assigning the managers
- Do these managers have the characteristics that are needed in implementing the strategy
- Is it better to bring in outsiders or use existing executives to implement the new strategy
- Can these managers handle larger spans of control

Criteria
- Personality and temperament
- Previous track record and experience
- Education
- Ability

11.3.3 Advantages of existing executives
- Insiders already know key people and conditions
- Insiders personal qualities are better known by associates
- Insiders have established relationships with peers, subordinates
- Employing insiders show the commitment to individual careers

11.3.4 Disadvantages of existing executives
- Less adaptable to major strategic changes
- The past commitment hinder the hard decisions required of a new strategy
- Have less ability to convey the need for change

11.3.5 Advantages of outsiders
- Outsiders may already believe in the new strategy
- Internal commitment to people wont burden outsiders
- Outsiders may have a stronger commitment and enthusiasm
- Bringing in outsiders clearly shows change is expected

11.3.6 Disadvantages of outsiders
- Costly of compensation and learning to work together time
- Uncertainty exist in selecting the right outsider

11.4 Defining the culture of an organization

Typical beliefs that shape organizational culture

- Being the best
- Having superior quality
- Believing that people are unique individuals
- Recognizing that customers are supreme
- Inspiring people to do their best

11.4.1 Impacts on a company culture

Implementation of a new strategy creates changes

Many key factors change and high compatibility of changes with the existing culture

The firm in cell one (Skillport job aid summary) is faced with carrying out a new strategy

This requires many changes in structure, systems and other aspects

Four considerations must be emphasized by these firms

- Link key changes to the company mission
- Place emphasize on the use of existing personnel
- Pay attention to the incompatible changes
- Pay attention to adjustments in the reward system

Few key factors change and high compatibility of changes with the existing culture

The firm in cell two (job aid summary) must emphasize two items

- Take advantage of the situation to reinforce and solidify the current culture
- Use this time of relative stability to remove organizational roadblocks to the desired culture

Few key factors change and low compatibility of changes with the existing culture

The firm in cell three (job aid summary) must make a few major changes to implement a new strategy, but these changes may not be compatible with its current culture

Many key factors change and low compatibility of changes with the existing culture

The firm in cell four (job aid summary) has a difficult time implementing their new strategies. They must make many changes that are incompatible with their current culture.

11.5   Establishing a reward system
Guidelines for a successful rewarding system
* Link rewards to the strategic plan
* Make incentives a major part of the compensation
* Link reward and incentives to each individual's job
* Reward individuals' performance and success
* Reward everyone and be sensitive to conflicts
* Reward fairly and accurately
* Generously reward a business's success
* Value a rewarding and motivating environment
* Be open to changing the reward systems

A detailed description is attached on the job aid summary regarding reward systems.

12. Strategic control and continuous improvement

Where are we going
How are we doing
Importance of strategic control
- Prevents problems when carrying out a strategy
- Solves problems during the whole process

12.1 Establishing strategic control
Four common ways to establish strategic control
- Premise control
- Implementation control
- Strategic surveillance
- Special alert control

12.1.1 Premise control
The premises of a strategy change over time
- Systematically check the validity of the premises on which the strategy is based
  - ✓ Environmental factors, inflation, technology
  - ✓ Industry factors, policy of competitors, substitute

- Process

The following steps are needed to check the process during the premise control
- Identify essential premises of a strategy during the planning process
- Assign the responsibilities for monitoring those premises for a qualified person
- Identify the premises that influence the strategy and make an adjustment on time

12.1.2 Implementation control
Transforms the planned strategy into detailed action
- Strategic thrusts, strategic components
- Milestones review

12.1.3 Strategic surveillance
An overall check of the functional aims that will influence the strategy
It surveys a wide range of events inside and outside a company

12.1.4 Strategic alert control
A method when unexpected events dramatically change a company's strategy

12.2   Operational control systems
This is a basis of strategy control
It controls activities to make sure they are being done as planned and it corrects any significant problems

Three types of operational control processes
- Budgets
- Schedules
- Essential success factors

12.2.1 Budgets
- Profit and loss
- Capital budgets
- Cash flow budgets

12.2.2 Schedules
- Giant chart, shows when each task is supposed to be done
- Flow chart, shows details about each task in a project

12.2.3 Essential success factors
Refer to the areas critical to carrying out strategies
- Identify critical elements
  - ✓ Quality of products
  - ✓ Service to the customer
  - ✓ Employee morale
  - ✓ Competition in the market

12.3   The quality imperative, continuous improvement
Quality is a never ending process
TQM = Total Quality Management, all staff members are involved

TQM is aimed at fulfilling the quality imperative
- C Client satisfaction
- C Correct measurement
- C Continuous improvement
- G Good working relationship

12.3.1 Ten important elements of TQM
- Specified quality
- Costumer orientation
- Detailed business process concentration
- Cooperation with clients and suppliers
- Problem prevention, ISO 9000
- Adoption of an error-free attitude
- Accurate measurement
- Employee participation
- Total involvement atmosphere
- Continuous improvement

13. Value Chain Analysis

This is a way to create competitive strategies that position a firm to gain and sustain marketplace advantage.

To create a sustainable competitive advantage, firms must provide greater values to buyers.

Values
➢ what buyers are willing to pay
➢ impact on buyer cost and performance
➢ evaluation of expected product performance relative to price
➢ worth of a product in exchange for other products

Steps to sustainable competitive advantage
➢ identify strengths which give your firm the best chance to win the competitive game
➢ offer products/services that distinguish your firm from others
➢ counter both direct and direct moves by rivals

Value chain refers to the set of activities linked together that enable a firm to create and deliver its product or services to the marketplace.

Activities vs. functions
➢ activities result in outputs which can be managed
➢ functions are a group of activities focusing on achieving the goals

Discrete activities (value activities) produce costs and creates values. This is the source of a firm's competitive advantage.

Categorizing activities in different ways helps to identify the issues, which create values to buyers
● relationship among various activities
● commonalities between activities
● impact of each activity on the firm's success

13.1   Generic categories
- a basic unit of work performed within an organization. Each activity is a physically and technologically distinct task a firm does.

Primary
- Inbound logistic
- Operations
- Outbound logistic (collecting, storing, distributing to buy)
- Marketing and sales
- Service

Secondary
- Firm infrastructure
- Human resources
- Technologically development
- Procurement (purchasing inputs for a firm's activities)

Primary activities consist the core of business and these actions create values, secondary activities don't create values by itself, they support the primary ones.

If the activity is involved in the production, creation, marketing/sales, distribution or support of the product/service, than it's a primary activity. Otherwise it's a secondary one.

13.2   Roles
Direct roles are immediately involved in creating values
Indirect roles enables direct activities to be performed. (quality assurance)

Factors
Every value activity (direct) employs and or creates
- ➢ purchased inputs, resources necessary to make products/services
- ➢ human resources, the personnel who provide the knowledge
- ➢ information, the collection of factors or data used to generate values
- ➢ technology, the equipment and approaches used to perform tasks
- ➢ assets and liabilities

Information can be either the input or output of a firm's value activities. Technology such as laboratory equipment, office automation, telecom equipment etc.

13.3   Assessment considerations
To define relevant activities, identify them based on two broad considerations
➢   technology, the type of equipment
➢   economics
   ✓   discrete economics
   ✓   factors related to economic or financial conditions
   ✓   impact on differentiation
   ✓   the role an activity plays in creating uniqueness in a firm's product
   ✓   or service. To different the product, service on the market
   ✓   significant or growing proportion of cost
   ✓   does the activity represent a significant or growing proportion of the cost

13.4   Linkages
Interrelate value activities and contribute to the influence of one activity on the cost or performance of another

It is critical to look for advantages in the interrelationship among strategically relevant activities

Horizontal
These are the interrelationships between value activities within a firm's value chain
◦   same function, different ways
◦   indirect efforts, direct improvements
◦   more work, fewer needs
◦   quality assurance
◦   mutual influence

Vertical
◦   Linkages between the firm and its suppliers

13.5 Buyer's value chain

For constructing the buyer's value chain it's important to look for not only how consumers use the products, but also every point of contact between the value chain and that of a buyer.

➤ Value assessment must be made from a buyer's point of view
➤ A buyer's view of value may change over time
➤ All parties involved in the purchase and use of a firm's products should be considered
➤ Analyzing a buyer's value chain can help a firm identify sources of cost advantage

13.6 Competitive scope

Several benefits
- determine how best to configure the value chain for maximum impact
- identify when and what kinds of coalitions might be useful
- strengthen the value chain and the competitive position

Dimension
- affect the competitive advantage with abroad, narrow focus

Segment
- vertical
- geographic
- industrial

Coalitions
- two types and how them impact a firm's competitive abilities

14. Cost advantage via value chain analysis

The target is to be the low cost provider in the marketplace.

A low cost provider is able to
- maneuver to under price competitors
- gain market share
- achieve higher profitability

To be low cost provider, two factors
- competitors of own value chain vs. others (what it does)
- relative cost of own activities vs. others (how much it cost)

14.1 Value chain for cost analysis
The nine generic categories in a value chain can be grouped in two ways
By type
- primary and secondary

by role
- direct, indirect, quality assurance

Direct activities are primary only
Indirect activities can be either primary or secondary. These activities must be assessed for their impact in adding value. If they don't, ask yourself "Why do them?"

If they add value you can ask the following questions
➤ "are they being done in the most efficient, cost effective way"
➤ "would they be better performed in another part of the organization or by an outside group"
➤ "how can they be modified to add greater value"

Quality assurance activities are secondary firm infrastructure activities
➤ "to what extent do they add value"
➤ "are they performed in the most cost-effective way"

➤ "what risk does the organization run if these activities are reduced or eliminated"
➤ "can activities be performed in ways that eliminate a need for quality assurance activities"

14.2   Disaggregating of a value chain

To create competitive cost advantages it's useful to assess activities that enables the firm to create significant advantages for the customers. These activities have specific cost impacts.

- lower cost
- improved performance
- "how does this activity contribute to customer value"
- "what would be the impact on customer value if it were eliminated"
- "do competitors perform the same activity to create customer value. If so, how. If not, why"

14.3   The principles to determine a particular activity impact

The size and growth of the cost represented by the activity
➤ it is used to focus attention on large and small cost
➤ it is used on growing cost elements that may change a firm's cost
➤ structure

The cost behavior of the activity
➤ it enables better to judge when to aggregate or disaggregate costs among activities

The competitor differences in performing the activity
➤ it requires examination of how a firm's competitors are performing similar activities

These 3 principles are used in disaggregating a value chain

14.4   Assignment of costs and assets

Operating costs are assigned to activities that incur them (raw materials—product)
Assets are assigned to activities that employ, control or influence their use.
Costs based on one activity can be assigned to this one.
Costs incurred by several activities must be allocated to each activity.

Assets value must be valued in a consistent way. There are 2 ways,
Book value
◉ Original value—depreciation
Replacement value
◉ Cost to replace the asset today

During the assignment of costs and assets, the time period should be chosen to minimize the effects of cyclical fluctuations or seasonality. The time period should be chosen to represent a firms performance over time.

14.5 Cost behavior
It refers to the way costs change along with changes in the factors that influence them. Cost drivers are the factors that cause costs. They determine how costs will change based on how activities are performed

Economic of sale
◉ refers to the condition when production facilities increase in size and capacity and production cost per unit decrease
Pattern of capacity utilization
◉ spreads fixed assets over a wider base of production
Learning
◉ refers to cost reductions form improved ability and procedures, independent of scale
Linkages
◉ refers to how the cost of an activity is affected by the performance of other value actions
Interrelationships
◉ means sharing value activities and know-how across the business units of a firm
Integration
◉ refers to the extent to which a firm performs a full array of functions, that is, integrates them into business
Timing
◉ is crucial for cost advantage, as sooner an fewer time, as better. Pioneer is the first player on a market, the later entrant is afterwards.
Discretionary policies

- value activity costs are often affected by policy choices, that reflect a firm's strategy. Selection of discretionary policy generally involves tradeoffs between cost and differentiation.

Location
- it might affect the cost of a particular value activity as well as its cost relative to other activities Institutional factors
- this refers to impacts as government regulations etc.

14.6   Diagnosis of cost drivers
Identify cost drivers
➤ examining the basic economics of an activity
➤ examining a firm's historical data
➤ interviews with experts
➤ comparing with competitors

Identify the interactions
➤ reinforcement, to gain a low cost position (expand)
➤ counteraction, made an effort to optimize the counteracting forces

14.7   Cost dynamics
Refers to how costs of activities change over time independent of the strategy

industry real growth, affects a firm's cost

differential scale, sensitivity can change the absolute and relative costs of value activities if there is a growth/decline of sales

different learning rate, may occur in a variation of relative costs

technologically change will affect relative costs, if they occurs at different rates among the activities

inflation hits cost elements in value activities

aging is an important source of cost dynamics

market forces often counteract initially favorable or unfavorable input costs

14.8   Cost strategy
Controlling cost
- Reconfiguring the value chain

Control cost drivers
- economics of sale
  - ✓ set policies to reinforce scale economies
  - ✓ exploit scale economies where the firm is favored
  - ✓ emphasize activities in which the firm has scale advantage
- learning
  - ✓ manage the learning curve
  - ✓ keep learning proprietary
  - ✓ learn from competitors
- effect of capacity utilization
  - ➢ level throughput
    - ✓ firms can increase average capacity utilization by smoothing out any fluctuations in volume throughout the value chain over time
    - ✓ reduce the penalty of throughput fluctuations
    - ✓ in order to avoid excess capacity you can create capacity for trend line demand, rather than year-to-year demand
- linkages
  - ✓ exploit linkages within the value chain
  - ✓ work with suppliers and channels to exploit vertical linkages
- interrelationships
  - ✓ share appropriate activities
  - ✓ transfer know-how
- integration / de-integration of departments
- timing
  - ✓ evaluate and exploit first mover advantage
  - ✓ evaluate and exploit late mover advantage
  - ✓ time purchases with the business cycle
- discretionary policies
  - ✓ identify the cost of policies and modify those that don't support
  - ✓ differentiation
  - ✓ invest aggressively in technology to develop low cost process
  - ✓ control optional expenses throughout the value chain

- location
- institutional factors

14.9 Reconfigure the value chain
- How can activities be linked differently to improve costs etc.
- How can an activity be done differently or eliminated if it doesn't add value
- What coalitions might lower or eliminate costs without harming value

Some ways to reconfigure your value chain
- implement more automation or a new process
- changing channels of distribution
- using different inputs
- innovate in vertical integration (forward, backward)
- changing the location
- using different communication ways

Cost benefits can accrue for two reasons
- reconfiguration restructures costs due to significant improvements in efficiency
- the basis of competition can be changed to favor a firm's strength

14.10 Pitfalls of cost leadership
- focusing only on manufacturing activities
- ignoring the cost of purchased inputs
- ignoring indirect or small activities
- misdiagnosis of cost drivers
- failure to understand and use linkages effectively
- contradictory cost reduction
- unintentional cross subsidy
- focusing on incremental improvements
- undermining differentiation

14.11 Benefits of cost strategy
- analyzing tradeoffs among alternative actions and their impact on value
- identifying the right actions to improve the firm's cost position relative to that of the rivals

15. Differentiation advantage via value chain analysis

If a firm creates features or processes that are difficult to imitate it often
- creates barriers to entry
- changes the nature of rivalry in the industry
- reduces the buying power of large buyers because substitutes are not
- attractive
- generates more sales, usually at higher prices
- attracts additional buyers and increases buyer loyalty

15.1   Sources of differentiation
Activities within a company value chain
- Breath of activities
  A number of ways exist to differentiate a firm through scope
  - geographic coverage
  - after sale receiving and support
  - one-stop shopping, single point of contact for buyers
  - one-stop service, single point of contact for service
  - compatibility among products in the product mix
- Channel activities
  - support
  - service
  - training

Establish standards for consistency in facilities, capabilities or image and choose channels accordingly
- Provide materials for channel use such as advertising, promotion and training
- Provide funding so that channels can offer credit

15.2   Drivers of uniqueness
- Policy choices
  - product mix, features and performance
  - range of services
  - technology deployment
  - personnel procedures

> ➤ quality of inputs and outputs
> ➤ skill and experience of personnel
> ➤ intensity and content of activities
> ➤ use of information
- Linkages
  > ➤ supplier linkages
  > ➤ channel linkages
- Timing
- Location
- Interrelationships, sharing of activities across business units
- Learning
- Integration level
- Scale, relates to the volume of business and its impact on unit costs
- Institutional factors

15.3 Differentiation costs
Scale, can reduce the cost, larger activity volume also brings better efficiency
Interrelationships
Learning, curve not only differentiate a firm but also lowers the cost of
    its production
Timing, impacts cost with respect to business cycles or market conditions

15.4   Buyer value and differentiation
A firm's activities comprise its value chain, a buyer's activity comprise
the buyer's value chain.
- Use of the product
- Direct, indirect impact
- Links between customer and firm

Buyer value sources
Firms create value for their buyers in two ways
- by lowering buyer cost
- by increasing buyer performance or satisfaction

Two kind of buyers
- organizational
- household

Two kind of costs
- financial, consumes less gasoline, save money
- non-financial, home delivery, saves time

How to lower buyer costs and increase buyer performance
- lower acquisition and maintenance costs, discounts
- lower direct usage costs, save service costs
- lower indirect usage costs, less training, better equipment
- lower rate of usage, less of the product is required
- lower costs unrelated to the product, free delivery service
- lower risk and cost of failure, improve the reliability

Opportunities to lower buyer costs
- tracing your product through the buyer's value chain
- identifying other products with which your product interfaces
- identifying other value activities of your firm and how they affect buyers

15.5 Buyer perception of value
It is often not easy to understand for buyers the value they have purchased
- What is the real value?
- How much is it (the price)

Signaling is important to expose unrecognized advantages of a firm's capabilities. When the following conditions prevail, signals of value are as important to differentiation as actual value created.

Buyer impact is subjective, intangible or hard to quantify
- Many people are first time buyers
- Buyers are quite unsophisticated
- Purchase is infrequent
- The price for a product will reflect real and perceived value.

Buyers pay only for value that they perceive, no matter how much value real exist. It's critical for a firm to signal its value effectively in order to command a premium price.

15.6   Buyer purchase criteria
There are five type of buyers in a purchasing process
- one who influences
- one who decides
- one who pays
- one who uses
- a channel

Purchasing criteria

use criteria, are ways in which a firm actually lowers cost or increases performance for buyers. These criteria define the price premium a firm can charge
- actual product
- delivery and support system
- product specifications
- consistency of meeting specifications
- intangibles
- downstream value

signaling criteria, are ways in which buyers judge or perceive the actual value they will receive. These criteria are valuable only when they contribute positively to the buyer's perception of the value of a product.
- advertising
- product and facilities appearance
- image and reputation
- market share
- price
- financial ability and business
- longevity

Signaling criteria are important when
- buyers have difficulty assessing a firm's performance
- a product is seldom purchased or a buyer is purchasing it for the first time
- buyers are relatively unsophisticated
- a product is custom designed and past experience doesn't fully represent future fulfillment

To identify new use criteria use several approaches
- developing knowledge of buyer needs
- making direct contact with buyers
- developing knowledge of the buyer's value chain and the linkages

There are three approaches into signals of value
- examining each use criteria for possible signals
- identifying every point of contact between a firm and its buyers
- analyzing a buyer's purchasing process

15.7   Increasing the value
To increase the value the following criteria must be existing
- precise and optional
- quantified if possible
- analyzed for effect on buyer cost and performance

15.8   Determining competitive positions
To determine the competitive position some key steps must be followed
- understand your competitor
- focus on critical success factors
- choose activities that offer the greatest value

Some questions about your competitor
- what are they offering
- what are their strengths
- what are their weaknesses

Value chain links in the following four areas are likely to produce an attractive longer lasting differentiation advantage
- technical superiority
- customer support services
- quality
- value for money

Firms must be aware that the remaining value to customers can' t easily be copied. When a firm is successful in creating such differentiation:
- creates barriers to entry
- changes the nature of rivalry in the industry

- reduces the buying power of large buyers because substitutes are not
- attractive
- generates more sales, usually at higher prices
- attracts additional buyers and increases buyer loyalty

15.9 Enhancing differentiation position
There are three basic ways
- perform existing value activity more uniquely
- create an advantage from the cost of differentiation
- reconfigure the value chain

Approaches to perform existing value
- assess every value activity for new ways to add value
- ensure that actual and intended product use are consistent
- employ effective signals of value
- bundle information with the product to ease both use and signaling

Approaches to create an advantage
- capitalize on all low cost sources of differentiation
- control cost drivers
- differentiate in areas where a firm has sustainable cost advantages
- lower cost in activities not related to differentiation

Approaches to reconfigure the value chain
- shift the decision maker

  a firm's value chain can be accomplished by modifying in the following ways
  - ✓ using technical people in the sales process
  - ✓ changing media and content of advertising or selling
  - ✓ materials
  - ✓ using a new type of salesperson
  - ✓ educating buyers about new decision criteria which
  - ✓ require a different decision maker
- identify unrecognized purchase criteria
- explore new ways to link the buyer's value chain with that of the firm

15.10 Sustainability of differentiation

- The firm sources of uniqueness involve barriers
- The firm has a cost advantage in differentiating
- The sources of differentiation are multiple
- A firm creates switching costs at the same time it differentiates

15.11 Pitfalls

There are some pitfalls which must be avoided if a firm want to be successful in differentiation

- Offering uniqueness that is not valued by buyers
- Providing too much differentiation
- Asking too high a price minimum
- Ignoring the need to signal value
- Not knowing the cost of differentiation
- Focusing on the product instead of the whole value chain
- Failing to recognize buyer segments

16. Focus advantage via value chain analysis

Foundation for industry segmentation
Different segments emerge if the following conditions exist
- cost of uniqueness drivers in a firm's value chain are affected
- the value chain configuration required for success is affected
- difference in the buyer's value chain are implied

Capture the most important differences
- what other ways on buyer value chain functions be performed using different technologies or designs?
- could enhanced capabilities enable additional functions to be performed?
- in what ways might productions be bundled to serve buyers better?

To identify differences among buyers and products, four classes of variables can be used
- varieties of products that are or might be produced and needs that are or might be fulfilled
- types of buyers and users that currently or potentially might purchase or use an industry's products
- alternative distribution channels that are used or might be used to reach end buyers
- geographically location of existing or potential buyers

16.1 Foundation for segmentation
Product variety
- tangible products
- services

Product varieties may be defined according to different dimensions
- size
- price
- features
- technology or design
- inputs

- packaging
- performance
- new vs. aftermarket or replacement
- product vs. additional services or equipment

Choose the most effective dimensions
Identify all product varieties

Product segments
- product types or varieties currently or potentially produced
- groups of products that might be packaged together

Buyer types
- business goods buyers, users
  - ✓ industry and strategy
  - ✓ technology
  - ✓ original equipment
  - ✓ vertical integration
  - ✓ decision making
  - ✓ size, ownership, finance
- consumer goods buyers, users
  - ✓ demographic
  - ✓ psychografic
  - ✓ language
  - ✓ decision making
  - ✓ purchase

Channel and location
Channels used by a firm plays two roles
- as a buyer representative of a firm's products
- as a link in its value system

Channels affect a firm's value chain
- exchange, buying and selling
- logistics, transportation and storage
- facilitating, financing, risk and market information

Channel participants
- agent
- wholesaler
- retailer
- broker
- manufacturer's agent
- distributor

geographic segments
- locations, regions, countries
- weather zones
- country's stage of development of other groupings

16.2   Segmentation process
Segmentation variables
The goal is to use only those variables that best fit your current position
- test each variable for value chain significance
- ➢ *Disaggregating the mass market!!*
  - ✓ Does it affect costs of value activities?
  - ✓ Does it affect the differentiation drivers?
  - ✓ Is it impacted by costs of value activities?
  - ✓ Is it impacted by the differentiation drivers?
  - ✓ Does it impact each of the five competitive forces?
  - ✓ Is it impacted by each of the forces of industry structure?
  - ✓ Is it important to customers?

Group similar variables
- Define the number of units for each variable

16.3   Segmentation matrix
- Create matrices using two variables
  some cells may have zero values, these are called null cells
- Identify the relationship among variables
  why are these variables related?
- Create combined matrices
  it is best to begin grouping variables within a category
  it is the foundation for strategic analysis
- Locate competitors on resulting matrices

16.4   Segmentation process illustration
- Identify all variables that impact or are be impacted
- Assess the significance of each variable
- Place the variables into meaningful categories
- Plot the variables on two-dimensional matrices and eliminate insignificant variables and null-cells
- Identify any correlated variables and select one to represent both
- Combine the matrices until one or only a few matrices remain with the most strategically significant variables
- Test the matrices by overlaying competitors activities

16.5   Segmentation and focus strategy
Choosing segments of the industry that you believe your firm has best serve against competitors

Attempt to achieve success through one of the two approaches
- differentiation focus exploiting special needs of buyers in some segments
- cost focus exploiting differences in cost behavior in some segments

16.6   Segment attractiveness factors
The appeal of a segment is dependent upon four factors

- The intensity of the five competitive forces in the segment
  - potential entrants
  - substitutes
  - rivalry
  - buyer power
  - supplier power

- The size and growth of the segment
  estimating the growth rate of various segments

- A firm's ability to meet the segment's need

- Interrelationships between the segment and others
  Benefits of sharing this means
  - lower cost
  - increased differentiation

Lucas Wiedemann

There are also some types of costs which must be considered
- cost of compromise
- cost of inflexibility
- cost of coordination

To find the interrelationships, look on the matrix

16.7 Focus strategy considerations
The basis for a focus strategy
The optimization of value chain

Two types of interrelationships
- segments in a given industry
- business units serving other industries

- The starting point of focus strategies
- The overlap of focus strategies
- The strength of a competitor
- The feasibility of a focus strategy
- Focus strategy may become feasible if
  - tailoring becomes less costly through ways such as improving economies on scale
  - segment growth is sufficient to overcome the fixed cost of serving it
  - scale thresholds of serving a segment are overcome by taking advantage of interrelationships with other segments
  - global pursuit of segment increases the volume of business and conquers scale of economies

16.8 Sustainability
Ability to compete against broadly targeted firms
Two factors determine the competitive advantage of a firm that focuses on a segment
- the broadly targeted firm must compromise to serve the focused segment
- while serving other segments
- the focus firm can shares value among the segments it serves

16.9   Pitfalls and opportunities

Compromise costs for competitors

- only when a broadly targeted competitor must sub-optimize in order to serve the focused segment does a competitive advantage for the focus firm *exist*

New ways of segmenting

- segmenting an industry in standard ways often conceals potential opportunities
- Bases for a broadly targeted strategy
- broadly targeted competitors can gain a competitive advantage only when the industry segments are quite similar and strong interrelationships exist among the segments

Excessive breadth of competitor's scope

- firms targeting a broad base of segments run the risk of being attacked by focusers because they may have to sub-optimize to serve many segments
- Changes in segmentation
- Implementation of new technology